put 9.50

W9-ASO-580

MARTHA COOPER

YOUR WORLD OF PETS

By Susan McGrath

Art by Barbara L. Gibson

BOOKS FOR WORLD EXPLORERS
NATIONAL GEOGRAPHIC SOCIETY

CONTENTS

4
YOU DON'T HAVE TO OWN IT 98

TITLE PAGE: *Stacey Bergin, 12, of New York City, gives her mixed-breed companion, O'Grady, a loving squeeze. Owning a pet as Stacey does can be one of the happiest experiences of your life.*

COVER: *You won't often see this unusual combination of pets—a puppy, a kitten, a parakeet, and a goldfish—together in one picture. Actually, the photographer made pictures of the animals separately and then put the pictures together. Is one of the animals shown here the pet for you?*

NATIONAL GEOGRAPHIC PHOTOGRAPHER JOSEPH H. BAILEY

1

OUT OF THE WILD

A dog whines and eagerly wags its tail. A cat quietly stalks a sparrow across the lawn. Both of these pets are acting like their wild relatives. Have you ever wondered how and when wild animals became part of the human household?

Scientists believe that humans began to tame animals some 12,000 years ago. At that time, people obtained food largely by hunting animals. Wolves probably followed the hunters, searching for meat the humans left behind. It's possible that one day a child looking for firewood stumbled across an orphaned wolf pup. The child might have taken the pup home and raised it as a pet. Over time, other wolves must have begun to live with humans.

That's how the whole process of domestication might have started. When the tame wolves had pups, people would have kept those they liked best: the biggest pups or the smallest, the strongest ones,

◁ *The last kind of wild horse alive today, Przewalski's (per-zhih-VAHL-skeez) horse lives only in captivity. Here, several graze in a preserve in Europe. All other "wild" horses are actually relatives of escaped tame horses.*

▷ *Many wildlife scientists believe that wolves, such as these three European wolves, are the ancestors of all pet dogs. Scientists say dogs didn't exist before 12,000 years ago. They believe humans at that time began to domesticate, or tame and breed, wolves. The results: the pet dogs of today.*

the friendliest ones, or the ones with the curliest tails.

After many generations of being tamed and bred, the wolves became domesticated. Many of them no longer looked much like their ancestors. Some were bigger. Some were smaller. Many had fur colors quite different from those of wolves.

By choosing and breeding early wolf-dogs with certain characteristics, humans created many breeds of dogs. Today there are about 150. Many scientists say all dog breeds—from delicate Chihuahuas (chuh-WAH-wahz) to wolflike huskies—are descendants of the wolf. Others believe another doglike animal, now extinct, is the ancestor of many breeds.

The wolf was probably the first animal to be domesticated. After wolves, people adopted many other animal companions. The newest addition to households is the gerbil—domesticated only 30 years ago.

A number of the animals people often enjoy as pets today probably started out not as people's companions but as handy meals. From studying bones uncovered in ancient dwellings, scientists know that horses were once an important source of food for humans. Old handwritten books tell of monks raising rabbits to eat on certain religious days. And, of course, people still raise cattle, chickens, and other animals for food.

Along the way, an especially warm bond developed between certain kinds of animals and their owners. These animals were so intelligent, friendly, loyal, or useful that people began to have second thoughts about eating them. These animals became pets.

Most pets have one thing in common: Their relatives in the wild live in groups. Wolves live in packs, horses and guinea pigs run in herds, goldfish swim in schools, and parrots fly in flocks. These animals were accustomed to companionship, so people found it easy to tame them. The animals transferred their

JANE BURTON/BRUCE COLEMAN LTD.

△ *People in China began to breed wild goldfish such as these more than a thousand years ago. Now pet goldfish swim in ponds and aquariums worldwide.*

▷ *Creature of the wild, a brown rat pauses at a meal. All pet rats are descended from the brown rat, even though many pet rats are black, white, or a mix of colors.*

6

© TOM MCHUGH/NAT'L AUDUBON SOC. COLL./PHOTO RESEARCHERS, INC.

Where in the world did the ancestors of modern pets live around the time they were first domesticated? In this map, each ancestor is represented by its profile in a circle or circles of one color. Check the key at the bottom of the map to find the color and profile of the animal you are interested in. You will see, for example, that a red circle represents the parakeet. Look for red circles on the map. You will find just one. Now you know that at the time people domesticated the parakeet, it lived in Australia.

◁ *A European rabbit peers from its burrow entrance. It shares its home with as many as 150 other rabbits. The European rabbit is tamed fairly easily. All domesticated bunnies were bred from it. North American rabbits, such as cottontails, are not tamed easily. They make poor pets.*

▷ *A cat called the African wildcat prowls among dry grasses. This animal is the direct ancestor of the house cat. Although the two look alike, the African wildcat is a bit larger. It lives in Africa, the Middle East, and southern Asia.*

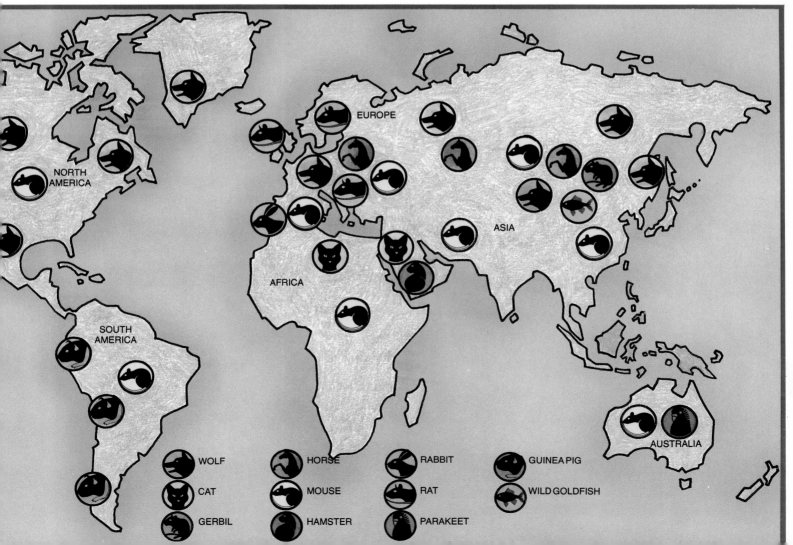

NORTH AMERICA

EUROPE

ASIA

AFRICA

SOUTH AMERICA

AUSTRALIA

WOLF

CAT

GERBIL

HORSE

MOUSE

HAMSTER

RABBIT

RAT

PARAKEET

GUINEA PIG

WILD GOLDFISH

loyalty from their group leaders to their new masters.

Not all pets of today once lived in groups, however. The ancestor of one familiar pet, the cat, has always lived and hunted alone. It's called the African wildcat.

Cats were first domesticated in Egypt, about 4,000 years ago. At that time, historians believe, African wildcats learned that villages were good places to catch mice and other rodents. At first, the cats hunted outside. Then they began to slip into houses. Happy to be rid of rodents, people probably welcomed the cats, and adopted orphaned kittens.

The new partnership grew. Today, there are millions of cat owners. Does it sometimes seem that cats think *they* are the owners, and people their guests?

△ *The taming of the wolf probably happened very gradually. This painting shows three ways that wolves might have grown used to humans. Hungry wolves in a pack, in the background, wait just outside the human camp. They have followed the humans* to pick up leftover scraps of meat when the people leave the camp. Closer in, a man offers meaty bones to a curious wolf and her pup. A child, at right, plays with a growing wolf pup that he found abandoned near its den. He is raising it as a pet.*

WERNER FORMAN ARCHIVE/BRITISH MUSEUM, LONDON

◁ *Ancient art provides clues to people and animals of the past. This 3,000-year-old stone carving shows a man grooming a horse much as people do it today. The art is part of a king's throne room in what is now the country of Iraq.*

▷ *A pet cat gnaws a bone in an Egyptian painting of 4,000 years ago. Egyptians, the first people to domesticate cats, worshiped a cat goddess. When a cat died, its owners shaved off their eyebrows to show their grief.*

ANDRÉ HELD CH-1024 EOUBLENS

PET HALL OF FAME

People don't preserve pet cats as mummies anymore, as they did in ancient Egypt. Some animal companions, however, do earn a permanent place in history. Animals become famous for many of the reasons people do—for performing heroic deeds or for doing something unusual or important. Here are seven candidates for what you might call the Pet Hall of Fame. Does a pet you know deserve a place?

10

1 *Igloo accompanied his master, explorer Richard Byrd, to the South Pole. The playful fox terrier kept Byrd and his companions so amused that they often forgot their icy surroundings.*

2 *A pioneer in the field of sight, Buddy became the first successful Seeing Eye dog. This skilled German shepherd proved to the world that dogs could be trained to see for blind people.*

3 Pussycat, a Maine coon cat, awakened her owners
in their burning house, allowing them to escape.
The heroic act earned her a bronze medal for bravery
and a certificate of merit from the ASPCA.*

4 Do you remember the grinning Cheshire cat in
Alice's Adventures in Wonderland? Lewis Carroll
wrote the story in 1865 for his friend Alice. Her cat
Dinah gave Carroll the idea for the Cheshire cat.

5 Charlotte the cockatoo went almost everywhere
with King George V of England. She even sailed on
his royal yacht. Whenever the king was away,
Charlotte would squawk, "Where's the captain?"

6 Confederate Gen. Robert E. Lee's beloved horse
Traveller carried him safely through the Civil
War. Traveller became more famous than he might
have liked. As the horse grazed, people sometimes
crept up and plucked souvenir hairs from his tail.

7 Almost 2,400 years ago, 12-year-old Alexander
tamed the stallion Bucephalas to impress his
father, the king of Macedonia. No other rider could
control the stallion. Riding Bucephalas, Alexander
the Great conquered much of the known world.

*ASPCA stands for the American Society for the Prevention of Cruelty to Animals.

11

2

WHAT PET SUITS YOU BEST?

Stacey Bergin wanted a pet. She had a lot of time and energy to devote to one. "But my father was allergic to cats, and my mother was scared of birds," says Stacey, 12, of New York City.

So what did she get? A mixed-breed puppy. Because Stacey lives in an apartment house on a busy street, she must walk her dog, O'Grady, at least twice a day. She trains him, feeds him, plays with him, and gives him a bath when he needs one. Stacey wouldn't trade O'Grady for any other animal in the world.

Choosing a pet that's just right for you is not easy. Each kind of pet has different needs. Each pet owner has different needs, too. If the pet's needs don't match up with the owner's needs, the owner—and the pet—can expect trouble. Before choosing a pet, take the time to find out what sort of animal will suit you best.

One of the first things to consider is how much room you can

◁ *Are you looking for a pet to join you in a small apartment? Birds, such as this pair of Gloster canaries, might be just the thing. Having two or more birds will keep them from becoming lonely.*

▷ *John Daub, 13, of Arlington, Virginia, enjoys playing hide-and-seek with his cat Petite. "The best thing a cat has to offer is company," says John. He and his sisters share Petite's companionship—and the work of taking care of her.*

12   HANS REINHARD/BRUCE COLEMAN LTD.   PAT LANZA FIELD

share with an animal. After all, you can keep fish in your bedroom, but you can't tie a pony to your dresser! If you live in an apartment, consider getting guinea pigs, cats, or birds. Such pets don't need much room to exercise. A dog can be a nuisance if you don't have a fenced yard—unless you're prepared to work as hard as Stacey does.

Before you get an animal, calculate how much time you'll have to spend caring for it and cleaning up after it. Aaron Dickens, 13, of Washington, D. C., figures that he spends an hour and a half each day with his hamsters. That includes playtime as well as work.

Make sure all the members of your family like the type of pet you've got your eye on. Are any family members allergic to cats? If you get a long-haired pet that sheds on furniture, will you be in big trouble?

Ask your family and your friends if they will help you look after a pet. Then if you leave school late, someone can walk or feed your pet for you. Ask yourself what you'll do about your pet during family trips.

Find out what it costs to buy and to care for the pet you want. Don't set your heart on one you can't afford. Pets bought from breeders may cost a lot. Some, such as large dogs, are expensive to feed. Remember, free or inexpensive pets adopted from shelters or from neighbors can be just as rewarding as expensive pets.

Do you spend much time at home every day? If you don't, buy an aquarium and keep fish. They won't be lonely when you go out. Do you like to stay in to read or to play games? You might like a warm cat to curl up with. Choose a companion, not a burden.

Prepare to love and to look after your pet all of its life—long after the kitten becomes a cat or the puppy becomes a dog. Choose a pet that needs the amount of care you can afford to give. Pick a pet that will give you joy long after its newness has worn off.

▷ *On a Pennsylvania farm, Carey Donches, 14, gives her lamb Sunshine a scrubbing. "You can't have a sheep—or a horse or pony— in a small area," says Carey. "Sheep and other farm animals need exercise, or they'll get flabby."*

△ *Fanning its colorful tail, a male guppy darts through its tank. If you live in an apartment, tropical fish may be particularly good pets for you. Start with inexpensive breeds such as the guppy before buying fancier fish.*

14

Stacey Bergin, 12, learned that owning a dog in the city is a big responsibility. She and her dog, O'Grady, live in New York City. She takes O'Grady out for a walk at least twice a day—in rain, snow, sleet, wind, or sunshine.

MARTHA COOPER

PET CARE RESPONSIBILITIES

	DOGS	CATS	BIRDS	FISH
HOUSING	Bed and kennel needed if outdoors. Bed needed if indoors.	Simple bed needed in a quiet place indoors.	Cage and perches needed. A large, wire-mesh–covered area called an aviary is desirable for birds kept outdoors in warm areas.	Aquarium is preferred. Large bowl is possible. Outdoor pool may be used for goldfish.
FOOD* (All pets should have fresh water at all times.)	Buy bagged or canned food at supermarket. Feed once a day.	Buy canned and boxed cat food at supermarket. Feed twice a day.	Buy birdseed at supermarket or pet store. Feed once a day—enough to last the whole day so bird will always have food available.	Buy fish food at supermarket or pet store. Feed once or twice a day.
GENERAL CARE AND GROOMING†	More than an hour a day. Brush long coats daily, short coats weekly. Bathe every three months, or as necessary.	More than half an hour a day. Brush long-haired cats daily. Brush short-haired cats twice a week.	About 20 minutes a day; much longer for birds you want to tame or teach to talk.	At least an hour a week. No grooming.
ATTENTION YOUR PET REQUIRES	High. Plan to spend several hours a day with your dog. Dogs enjoy companionship and playing—both indoors and out.	Medium. The more time you spend playing with a cat, the more affectionate it is likely to be. Having two cats helps keep them from being lonely when you're away.	Medium. Birds seem happiest with some company. Having two helps keep them from becoming lonely.	Low. For the sake of the fish, it's best to have at least two of them.
LIFE SPAN	At least 10 years for most.	At least 10 years for most.	5 to 60 or more years, depending on breed of bird. Parakeets: 6. Parrots: 60 or more. Canaries: 5–10 years.	2–10 years.
VET CARE	Regular: twice a year after first visit, plus visits for worming and for neutering or spaying.	About two visits for a kitten. Then, once a year, plus a visit for neutering or spaying and visits for worming.	When ill, and to trim beaks and nails if necessary. Birds provided with proper cage equipment usually keep their beaks and nails in shape by themselves.	Only when ill.
EXPENSES FOR CARE	Medium.	Medium.	Low.	Medium to low.

16   *For adult animals only. The young may have different requirements.   †Daily times given are minimums.

Are you having trouble deciding what kind of pet to choose? There are many facts and figures to consider. This chart about pet care and expenses may help you out. The categories of information are listed down the left side of the chart. The different animals appear across the top. Find a pet that interests you, then read directly below it to get information about the animal. To compare pets, read across the rows.

HORSES AND PONIES	RATS AND MICE	GERBILS	HAMSTERS	RABBITS	GUINEA PIGS
Fenced pasture or paddock needed. Stable or barn necessary for shelter.	Cage needed. Best to use a dry aquarium or a cage with wire-mesh walls (not a bird cage).	Cage needed. Best to use a dry aquarium or a cage with wire-mesh walls (not a bird cage).	Cage needed. Best to use a dry aquarium or a cage with wire-mesh walls (not a bird cage).	Indoor cage or weatherproof outdoor cage needed.	Cage needed. Best to use a dry aquarium or a cage with wire-mesh walls (not a bird cage).
Buy hay from farmers, grain at feed store. Feed and water twice a day at regular times.	Buy pellets at pet or food store. Feed enough so that food is always available.	Buy pellets at pet or food store. Feed enough so that food is always available.	Buy pellets at pet or food store. Feed enough so that food is always available.	Buy pellets at pet or food store. Add grass cuttings and hay. Feed once a day.	Buy pellets at pet or food store. Add hay. Feed once a day.
At least an hour and a half a day for feeding, cleaning, grooming, and exercising.	About half an hour a day. Clean cage daily for mice, once a week for rats. No grooming.	About half an hour a day. Clean cage once a week. No grooming.	About half an hour a day. Clean cage once a week. No grooming.	At least half an hour a day. Clean cage once a week. Groom once a week for short-haired; daily for long-haired.	About half an hour a day. Clean cage daily.
High. Ride a horse often. Clean hooves and groom daily. Best to have two to keep the animals from being lonely.	Medium. Rats more easily tamed than mice. Both friendly to people. Have at least two so they won't be lonely.	Medium. Easily tamed, and friendly. Handle pet daily to keep it tame. Own two so they can keep each other company.	Low. Best to keep caged singly. Handle often to keep tame. No grooming.	High. Hold and pet your rabbits often, or they will become less tame. Females make good companions for each other.	Medium. As friendly as gerbils; not as playful. Buy two so they have company. Long-haired needs brushing often.
20–35 years.	3–4 years.	1–5 years.	1–4 years.	5–10 years.	4–5 years.
Regular: twice a year, plus frequent visits from a farrier, or blacksmith, for care of hooves.	Only when ill.	Only when ill.	Only when ill.	Only when ill.	Only when ill.
High.	Low.	Low.	Low.	Low.	Low.

PET-PROOFING YOUR HOME

WRONG!

1. Fido eyes his tempting choices: Will it be the garbage or the bottle marked as poisonous? Kitty inspects the open cupboard before knocking a glass onto the floor and cutting her paw on a knife by the sink.

2. Now in the bathroom, Kitty licks a few medicine bottles. She'll knock over some cleaning fluid, then fall into the toilet. Luckily, she's big enough to rescue herself.

3. Ready for a nap, Kitty climbs into a warm dryer. You'd better hope no one turns it on. Next she'll use the washer for hide-and-seek and fling some detergent around, just for the fun of it.

4. You left Chewy the hamster in the sun, and he's starting to heat up. You'd better come back soon! Polly thought the mirror was an open window and knocked herself out.

5. A cheerful wag of Fido's tail sends a low plant flying. Kitty is shredding the sofa and may start chewing on that tempting lamp cord. If she isn't electrocuted, she'll take a stroll through the open fireplace. Kitty might someday be in for a hot surprise.

6. Fido has found an open gate. He's looking for adventure. Do you think he'll cross the street safely? How far will he wander—and will he come back?

18

You've made the big decision and picked out a pet that's perfect for you. Right away, there are a number of things you and your family can do to help make your home safe for your new pet. Just as important for your family's peace of mind, there are ways to keep your home safe *from* your pet. Before the pet moves in, take a good look at your home through your pet's eyes. Is it pet-proof?

RIGHT!

1. *Fido eagerly glances around the kitchen, but you've closed the cupboard doors and put away the garbage. He knows he'll find his own private supply of food in his dog dish. Kitty happily scratches an itch. She's been trained to stay off the counter and the stove.*

2. *Kitty looks around the bathroom. The cabinets are shut; the toilet lid is down. Perhaps just a catnap is in order.*

3. *The laundry room looks pretty dull with all those closed doors. Kitty does what you're supposed to do in the laundry room—a little washing up.*

4. *Cool, calm, and collected, Chewy rests in the shade. Polly sits on her perch and will entertain Chewy with a squawky song. Next time you let Polly out, hang a towel over the mirror so she won't take it for an open window.*

5. *Fido naps comfortably while Kitty sharpens her claws on her new scratching post. You've coiled the lamp cord, screened off the fireplace, and hung the plant out of reach. Did you know that many house-plants are poisonous to pets?*

6. *Admiring the scenery, Fido stays safely behind the closed gate and out of trouble. He'll love a walk on a leash when you come home.*

19

3

CARING FOR YOUR PET

There's no such thing as a recipe for pet care. But if there were, pet owners would agree on one important ingredient. "It's love," says Dawn Milligan, 11, of Georgetown, South Carolina. "Give your pet a lot of attention, and it will love you back."

Pets that come from warm, loving homes are usually happier and healthier than pets left to live mostly on their own. Pets from loving homes may live longer, too. However, there is more to pet care than just affection.

"A pet cannot live only on love," warns Dr. Michael Fox, a veterinarian in Washington, D. C. "In some ways, owning a pet is like being a parent," he says. "Pets need care. Each kind of animal has needs, and it's important to learn what those needs are." This chapter will tell you how to care for your animal companion—whether it's a dog, cat, guinea pig, horse, fish, rodent, rabbit, or bird.

◁ Milo, a German shepherd mix, gets a bath from Whitney McBee, 14, of Arlington, Virginia. Whitney noticed Milo scratching and discovered that an army of fleas had moved in. Watch your pet closely so you can tell if it needs help getting rid of fleas—or if it has other problems.

▷ Dawn Milligan, 11, of Georgetown, South Carolina, rewards her cockatiel, Cookie, with a birdseed treat. Dawn is teaching the bird to jump from her hand to her shoulder. "Cookie likes attention," says Dawn.

SUSAN T. MCELHINNEY

DAVE HORNBACK

HOW TO PICK A HEALTHY PET

DOGS

If you're picking out a puppy, sit down quietly with the litter. Does one of the livelier puppies appeal to you most? Choose the one that does. It's best to pick a puppy that shows interest in you and seems unafraid. Also look for

- a friendly personality

- bright, clear eyes

- clean, shiny skin inside the ears

- either a wet or a dry nose that's cool

- a strong, solid body; smooth, regular breathing; and fresh breath

- a clean, glossy coat and healthy-looking skin

- white teeth and firm, pink gums

- a good appetite

CATS

Decide on a kitten or a cat the same way you'd decide on a puppy. Take one that wants to play. Spend some time with your choices and pick the one that seems just right to you. Look for

- a lively, curious personality and fast reflexes

- smooth, regular breathing and fresh breath

- clean skin inside the ears, free of black, cakey accumulations

- a dry, clean, and cool nose

- a full coat, and skin that's clear of flakes

- firm, pink gums and white teeth

- bright, clear eyes

- a kitten or a cat that doesn't scratch itself or sneeze frequently

- a kitten not less than six weeks old

FISH

When buying fish, you'll be choosing from tanks with many fish in them. Look over all the fish in a tank. If several are dead or look diseased, choose fish from another tank. If the fish you want don't seem healthy, go to a different store. Look for

- bright eyes that aren't sunken

- a fish with no sores, white fuzzy patches, lumps, or missing scales

- whole fins with no marks or scraggly edges

- a fish that swims smoothly and upright

- a fish that doesn't seem to be gasping (unless you're buying an air breather, such as a gourami)

HORSES AND PONIES

Don't be in a hurry when you choose a horse or pony. Spend quiet time with the animal to get to know its personality. Watch someone else ride the horse, and then ride it yourself. Before making the final decision, have a vet examine the horse to make sure it's healthy. Look for

- strong legs

- a calm disposition

- regular breathing

- smooth, uncracked hooves

- a smooth, glossy coat with no sores or scars

- a horse that is neither too fat nor too thin

- healthy teeth, clear eyes, and a dry nose

RABBITS, MICE, RATS, HAMSTERS, GUINEA PIGS, AND GERBILS

Among these pets, it's hard to tell which individual will have a friendly personality. Most will scramble away from you at first, but a healthy baby rat might wander over to investigate you. Choose rodents that are about a month old. They will be easier to tame than older ones. Look for

- clean ears

- bright eyes

- a clean tail area

- a smooth, glossy coat

- a strong, solid-feeling body

- a nose that isn't runny or stuffy

- an alert appearance

BIRDS

If possible, buy a young bird—one that is about eight weeks out of the nest. Young birds are easier to tame than full-grown birds, and they are more likely to become attached to their owners. Look for

- an active, alert appearance

- clean feathers under the tail

- smooth, sleek plumage with no bare spots and no ruffled or broken feathers

- a bird that stands firmly on its legs

- a beak and claws that are not overgrown

- clean nostrils at the top of the beak

DOGS

Whether you got your new dog from a neighbor, a breeder, a pet shop, or an animal shelter, schedule a visit to the veterinarian right away. The dog will need vaccinations and should have a checkup. Start out right—with a healthy pet.

Feel free to ask the vet for advice while you are there. What kind of dog food does the vet recommend? The most costly brands may not be the best.

Puppies eat often—four times a day when they are very young. Their small stomachs become bloated if they eat too much at once. To get the nourishment they need, puppies should eat small meals, and many of them. Adult dogs need only one full meal a day.

A dog likes routine. Feed it the same kind of food at the same time in the same place every day. Don't feed it cat food. That has what cats need, not dogs. Provide a bone occasionally, but only a big beef bone. Small or soft bones splinter and can stab a dog's insides.

Make sure your dog has a warm place to sleep. When it goes there for a little peace and quiet, leave it

◁ *Three Yorkshire terriers show how the breed's colors change with age. Puppies have mostly black hair. Adults are largely golden brown. They grow blue-black hair on the back. These small dogs require combing and brushing daily. Some owners tie a Yorkie's hair in a little ponytail to keep it out of the dog's eyes.*

alone. If the dog wants any company, you'll know!

Brush your dog regularly. Don't make grooming a game. If your dog jumps around and tries to grab the brush with its teeth, you'll have a hard time brushing.

You don't have to bathe your dog often—only when it is particularly smelly or when it has fleas. Ask your vet about dips, sprays, powders, and other remedies designed to get rid of fleas.

One of your most important jobs as a dog owner will be to train your pet. Start housebreaking it right away. Watch to see when it whines, or sniffs in circles. These are often signs that it has to relieve itself. Rush the pup to newspapers, to a litter tray, or outside. Then praise it. Most puppies soon catch on.

When you bring your puppy home, teach it the commands "No!" and "Drop it!" You'll see the need for these the first time your pooch runs off with your shoe or carries a dead fish home from the beach.

When your dog is about ten weeks old, teach it these simple commands: "Sit!" "Stay!" "Down!" and "Come!" If your dog doesn't come right away when you call it, don't be cross. Coax it toward you in a friendly manner and repeat the command calmly until it obeys you. Then praise and pet the puppy.

Unless you plan to be a professional breeder, have your dog operated on so that it cannot breed. This is called neutering (for males) or spaying (for females). The operations are simple and make life easier for you and your dog. Spayed females won't attract males and be pestered by them. Once a male is neutered, it will fight less often and may be less likely to wander.

And finally, here's the biggest job for a dog owner: Make sure your pet gets enough exercise. Most dogs need a lot of exercise. It's good for people, too. Take your dog on two lengthy walks a day—rain or shine.

STEPHEN GREEN-ARMYTAGE

◁ *A lively Jack Russell terrier makes a flying catch. Playing fetch is fun for both you and your pet. It gives your dog plenty of exercise— and it helps keep you in shape, too.*

DAVID FALCONER/BRUCE COLEMAN INC.

△ *Known as a snowshoe foot, a husky's paw has fur and tough pads. It's well suited to ice and snow. Examine your dog's foot. Is it as protected as the husky's?*

▷ *A shake sends water flying. The dog seems to twist in two directions at once because its skin fits loosely. When a dog shakes, the skin at its shoulders moves first, followed by the skin at the rear.*

JOHN ANGELL GRANT/BRUCE COLEMAN INC.

▷ *A vet checks a cocker-poodle mix. Regular visits to the vet, twice a year, can help keep your dog healthy. Take a new dog in for a checkup right away.*

▽ *Your dog should have a tag like this to show that it has been vaccinated against rabies. Add a tag with your address and phone number in case your dog is lost.*

TOM PORTER

MARTHA COOPER

△ *At an obedience class in New York City, Lenny Bednarz, 12, teaches Becky to heel. Instructor Micky Niego stresses the importance of training. It can make the difference between a popular and an unpopular dog.*

28

▷ *As Micky watches, Lenny trains Becky to sit. "I pulled up on her collar, stroked her back, and pushed down while talking to her nicely," says Lenny. "Becky didn't obey 'Sit!' but when I stroked her back she sat down right away."*

MARTHA COOPER (ABOVE AND RIGHT)

TIP-TOP TIPS

▽ Buy a good leash and start an exercise program for your dog and yourself. A nylon leash, about 6 feet (2 m) long, is best.* This length allows your pet to walk comfortably in front of you. Don't ride your bike with your dog on a leash. You both might get hurt.

△ Did a skunk spray your dog? A bath of tomato juice will help take the smell away. Let the tomato juice dry on the dog's coat, then brush it out.

▽ Never leave your dog alone in a car on a hot day—even with the windows open a bit. In warm weather, the air inside a parked car heats up rapidly. A dog must be able to pant cool air to keep cool. It can die from too much heat in only 20 minutes. Make sure your pet always has fresh air.

△ Are you taking a trip with your dog? Pack a pet travel kit. Include the dog's dishes, a supply of food and water, a sleeping pad, a brush, and a favorite toy.

▽ Be smart about dog toys. Provide a leather or nylon "bone" for chewing, or a tennis ball tied inside a sock. Don't give a dog toys it can chew apart and swallow.

▷ You don't have to be romping with a dog or throwing it a stick to enjoy its company. Kelly Ryan Hurst, 13, of Auburn, California, frequently enjoys the restful companionship of Omi, a Samoyed (SAM-uh-yed). Quiet moments can strengthen the bond between you and your dog.

*Metric figures in this book have been rounded off.

ROBERT PEARCY

30

Pointers were named for their ability to point out birds to hunters. They are extremely active dogs and need a lot of exercise.

N.G.S. PHOTOGRAPHER JAMES L. STANFIELD

ROBERT PEARCY

BREEDS

How many species of dogs have you seen during your lifetime? Twenty? Fifty? Wrong! There is only one species of dog. That means that a dog such as the silky, long-haired Afghan can mate with a dog as different as the curly, wire-haired Airedale. There are, however, more than 150 *breeds* of dogs.

People bred most kinds of dogs for particular purposes: huskies to pull sleds, terriers to chase animals down holes, spaniels to carry game birds. Most breeds have personalities that go along with their uses. Hunting dogs like to chase things. Guard dogs often dislike strangers. Mutts, or mixed-breeds, may combine traits of both parents. If you know what a mutt's parents were, you can guess at its personality type.

△ *This puppy belongs to the world's favorite—and largest—group of dogs: the mutt. A mutt, or mixed-breed, can make a fine pet.*

S. C. BISSEROT/BRUCE COLEMAN INC.

△ *The easygoing Labrador retriever makes a good family dog. Labs—black, yellow, or brown—need plenty of exercise.*

▷ *Could you guess that these tiny toy poodles' ancestors were rough-and-tumble hunting dogs?*

JEAN-PAUL FERRERO/ARDEA LONDON

33

Resting beside its littermate, a chow chow puppy shows its blue-black tongue. Only one other dog breed, the Chinese Shar-Pei, has a tongue as dark as this. People in China bred the chow chow for such activities as hunting, pulling sleds, and guarding homes. Like other guard dogs, this breed is often unfriendly to strangers but playful with its owners.

ROBERT PEARCY

CATS

Some people think that cats are independent and maybe even standoffish. But if you've ever lived with a properly brought up cat, you know that isn't always so. Given a lot of care, most cats will be playful, loyal, and affectionate companions.

The first months are especially important for your kitten. Pay plenty of attention to it during this time. Play with it, brush it, settle down and hold it in your lap. The more time you spend with a kitten, the more friendly it will be as a cat. Treat your kitten as a companion and it will be a cat companion for life.

Take your new cat to the vet for its first checkup right away. The vet will examine it for signs of illness and will check it for worms. The vet will also give your cat shots. They will protect your pet against diseases such as distemper and rabies.

Back at home with your healthy cat, look around and choose a good place for its bed. A warm, quiet spot away from human traffic is best. The bed itself doesn't have to be fancy. A cardboard box raised off

◁ *Cuddling for warmth and company, tabby kittens rest in the sun. "Tabby" is the name of the common house cat with patterned fur. The name comes from a wavy-patterned Middle Eastern silk, called* atabi. *Long whiskers, near the mouth and above the eyes, help cats feel their way in the dark.*

the floor with a cushion in it makes a fine cat bed.

Feed your cat on a regular schedule. If you have a kitten, make sure it has dry kitten food available at all times, and feed it canned food two or three times a day. After the cat is six months old, feed it twice a day. It's best to give it both canned and dry food, in separate bowls. Either dry or canned food alone may make your cat sick. Occasionally add vegetables, cottage cheese, and cooked meat or fish. Don't give your cat milk. It may cause an upset stomach.

Always serve food at room temperature. If you take food from the refrigerator, let it warm up or add a little warm water before giving it to your cat.

Use a shallow bowl for food. A cat doesn't like to poke its head into a deep bowl. Make sure the cat always has plenty of water. Change the water daily.

Some cats may drink from toilet bowls. This is a dangerous habit. A kitten or even a cat can fall in and drown. Keep toilet lids down. Potted plants are another source of danger. Many houseplants are poisonous to cats. Hang them out of a cat's reach. (It *is* safe to grow potted grass for your cat to nibble on.)

Before you bring your new cat home, prepare a litter pan for it. Buy litter and a plastic pan at a pet store or supermarket. If you prefer, tear up newspaper or use sand to fill the pan. Place the pan in a private spot out of people's way.

Cats are tidy. Most don't have to be trained to use a litter pan. They simply have to know where the pan is. Take your new cat to the litter pan as soon as you get home. Place it in the pan and rustle its paws in the litter. The cat should get the idea right away.

Occasionally, a cat does not immediately learn to use a litter pan. If this happens, place the cat and a litter pan in a holding pen or in a small room. Keep the

 The pupils of a cat's eyes narrow into slits to close out bright light. In dim light, the pupils widen into full circles.

◁ *Two-day-old kittens drink their mother's milk. Kittens' eyes, closed at birth, do not open for about ten days. If your cat has kittens, give the new family plenty of privacy. Speak softly to the mother. Don't handle the kittens more than necessary.*

△ *A house cat pounces on prey much as its wild relatives do. If your cat goes outdoors, protect the birds around your home. Put a bell on the cat's collar to alert the birds. Make sure the collar has elastic in it so it will slip off if it should catch on a branch.*

A lick from a cat's tongue is like a sandpaper rub. Tiny spikes called papillae (puh-PIH-lee) cover the tongue. They comb a cat's fur, scrape meat off bones, and help a cat lap up a drink.

HANS REINHARD/BRUCE COLEMAN LTD.

cat there for a few days. This isn't punishment. Spend time playing with your pet, but keep it shut in—and don't clean up after it. A cat can't stand a mess. It will start to use the pan. After it does, leave the cat there one or two more days. Then your pet should be trained and you can let it roam the rest of your house.

Once the litter pan is used, keep the litter as clean as possible. Take out solid waste every day. Discard the litter and scrub the pan with warm water and baking soda twice a week. The baking soda will help prevent the pan from having an unpleasant odor.

If you're thinking about letting your cat breed, keep in mind that there are already many kittens in the world that have no home. You can help keep down the number of homeless kittens by taking your pet to the vet for an operation. The operation is called neutering (for males) or spaying (for females). It will prevent your cat from breeding. The operation is simple and safe. It won't harm your pet's personality. In fact, your cat will probably be a happier house pet after the operation—and you'll have done your share in keeping down the population of homeless kittens.

◁ *Grant Karcher, 9, of Brighton, Michigan, combs Peaches. Grooming helps to remove loose hairs from a cat's coat. Short-haired cats, such as Peaches, do not need much grooming, but they enjoy the attention. Long-haired cats should be combed daily.*

◁ *Dr. Judy Garland listens to a kitten's heartbeat. "It is important to bring a new kitten in for a checkup right away," says Dr. Garland, of Arlington, Virginia. "If the kitten is ill, you can usually treat it so that it will become healthy." A cat should return to the vet at least once a year for shots against diseases.*

Twice a week, Grant empties ▷ *his cat's litter pan and scrubs it out. He scoops solid waste from it every day. These few minutes of work help keep Peaches—and the house—clean and fresh.*

△ *Grant spoons out cat food for Peaches. He feeds the cat both canned and dry foods in the morning and again in the evening.*

41

TIP-TOP TIPS

▽ Cut all loops in curtain cords and cords for blinds. Straight cords are less likely to entangle a pet than loops. If the cords are straight with plastic tips, remove the tips. A cat may chew them and swallow splinters.

▷ Is your cat up a tree? Try using bait to coax it down. Open a can of tuna fish or cat food or get a very smelly fish. Hold this bait at the base of the tree. When your cat smells the food, it should soon come down the tree.

◁ Build your cat a jungle gym for exercise and for use as a scratching post. Attach a tall wooden post to a plywood base. Secure the post near the top to a wall or to the ceiling. Use plywood and brackets for shelves on the sides. Cover the post and shelves with carpeting. Your cat will enjoy scratching the post and climbing about on it. The cat will jump from shelf to shelf, and rest high up with a bird's-eye view of the room. Your cat may like its tower so much that it may even stay off the furniture.

△ Play hide-and-seek with your cat. Tie a cat toy to a long string and hide the toy under a blanket on the floor. Tug the string to make the toy move, tempting the cat to pounce on it.

△ Your cat has a body language that you can learn to understand. Can you tell what messages these cats are sending? The cat on its back, exposing its tender belly, is showing trust and asking to be petted. The other, with its back arched and hair on end, is frightened and is hissing a warning. Watch your cat closely in a variety of situations. You'll learn to tell what it's "saying."

▷ John Daub dangles a toy on a string for Mittens. Cats are extremely playful. Playing with your cat will usually make it respond to you better. Make a toy like this one. The cat will attack it as if the toy were a mouse. After playing with string or yarn, put it away—out of your cat's reach. A cat can easily entangle itself and be choked by loose string.

PAT LANZA FIELD

The Maine coon cat, an American breed, is noted for its large size and its gentleness. It's also known for its tail, which is so bushy that people once believed the Maine coon cat was part raccoon.

J. SHERWOOD CHALMERS

BREEDS

If you saw all 37 breeds of cats at a cat show, you might be surprised at how much they look alike. You know that most dog breeds have obvious differences. But to nonexperts, many cat breeds look similar. Even wild cats, such as leopards, have the basic shape and movements of a house cat.

The differences among cat breeds show up mostly in their colors, their markings, and the length of their fur. Breeders try to develop cats with exact characteristics—a set distance between the eyes, fur of a certain length, eye color that is just so.

Pet owners aren't usually so particular. Many are happy with the most common breed of all, the domestic shorthair—also known as the alley cat.

△ *A mixed-breed cat such as this calico-colored kitten usually makes a lively pet. Most calico, or three-colored, cats are female.*

△ *Not all mixed-breed cats have short hair. This orange tabby has a ruff like a lion's mane.*

▷ *The Burmese, a breed that comes in several shades, can make a fine pet as well as a show cat.*

Seal point Siamese kittens show the solid cream color typical of Siamese cats their age. As they grow older, their paws, legs, tails, ears, and faces will darken to a color called seal point—the seal-brown color their mother has. The Siamese breed was first developed in the Kingdom of Siam, now Thailand.

46

RABBITS AND GUINEA PIGS

Rabbits and guinea pigs have a lot in common. Although they're not members of the same animal family, they eat similar foods, they need similar kinds of care, and they both make good pets. This section will tell you how to care for both kinds of pets.

The first thing a rabbit or a guinea pig needs is a hutch, or house. The best possible hutch has two rooms—a dark sleeping room with plenty of hay, and a larger room for playing and exercising. Guinea pigs may use solid floors, but rabbits should have floors of closely woven wire mesh. You can keep guinea pigs in a large glass tank with a small cardboard sleeping room inside. Spread newspaper on the bottom of the hutch or tank. Cover it with wood shavings or hay.

A rabbit usually leaves its droppings in one corner. Put a litter tray there, and the rabbit may use it. Clean a rabbit's hutch once a week. A guinea pig isn't so tidy. It leaves droppings wherever it happens to be, so you'll have to clean its house daily.

Rabbits often eat their own droppings. Don't be

◁ *"You should always hold a guinea pig in a position so that it feels support," says Jennifer Shepherd, 12, of McLean, Virginia. Jennifer lifts her guinea pig's heavy hindquarters with one hand while holding its shoulders steady with the other.*

49

alarmed. When they do this, they take in the vitamins that bacteria in their droppings help to manufacture.

Unless you live in a very cold part of the world, keep your rabbit hutch in a garage or outdoors. Except in warm climates, keep guinea pigs indoors. Build legs onto the hutch or place the pet's home on a secure stand or table to keep your animals away from cats and dogs. Don't leave rabbits or guinea pigs in direct sunlight, in drafty, cold areas, or in damp spots.

In the wild, guinea pigs live together peacefully, as do rabbits. As pets, guinea pigs still live together peacefully, but not all rabbits do. Two females will get along; two males won't. And if you keep a male and a female together, you'll soon have a lot of young.

Feed pellets to your rabbit or guinea pig once a day. Always give guinea pigs hay or grass trimmings with their pellets. Rabbits eat hay, too, but it is not so important to their diet. Make sure the grass you cut has no weed killer on it. The poison can make your pet ill.

Guinea pigs need more vitamin C than most kinds of pellets provide. To be safe, feed guinea pigs small amounts of potato skins or lettuce every day, or give them extra vitamin C by adding it to their water. You can get vitamin drops at a pet store.

A small ceramic dog dish makes a good food dish for hutch animals. Give them water in a gravity water bottle, which you can buy at any pet store. A gravity water bottle hangs upside down on the cage. It has a metal spout from which the animal sips water.

Play with a young rabbit or guinea pig gently and as often as you can. It will become a fine companion. Never pick up a rabbit by the ears. This hurts it and can damage the ears. A guinea pig handled frequently may learn tricks such as "Sit-up-and-beg" and "Shake!" A well-brought-up rabbit will often enjoy a gentle game of tag.

△ *Jackie Weber, 10, of Canton, Ohio, cuddles her black Dutch bunnies. Hold and pet your rabbits or guinea pigs often, especially when they are young, and they will become warm and friendly companions.*

▽ *At a rabbit show in Ohio, Jackie watches as a judge inspects her ribbon-winning mini-lop rabbit. A mini-lop's ears hang down. The judge looks at such things as the shape of the ears, how full the coat is, and how quietly the rabbit sits.*

▷ *Jennifer adds cedar chips to her guinea pig's tank. A cage for a guinea pig should have a solid floor or a floor of closely woven wire mesh. Clean the cage daily, then spread newspaper and add a layer of cedar or pine chips.*

TERRY EILER (LEFT AND BELOW)   PAT LANZA FIELD (OPPOSITE)

50

TIP-TOP TIPS

△ Never put a rabbit or a guinea pig in a room with a TV on. High-frequency sounds from the set—so high that people can't hear them—will hurt your pet's ears.

▽ Does your rabbit or guinea pig want a treat? Dry bread is just the thing. Your pet will enjoy this crunchy food, which otherwise might be thrown away.

▽ Guinea pigs like to explore dark spaces. Put a cardboard box in the cage, or make a tunnel by cutting the toe off a sock and taping the other end around a section of a wide mailing tube. Rabbits

▷ Learn to read your rabbit's body language. If your bunny nudges you with its muzzle, it wants attention. If it stretches out on its tummy, lays back its ears, and lets its eyelids droop, it's through playing. It wants to rest. If your rabbit tenses up, lays back its ears, raises its tail, or thumps a hind foot, you've got an angry rabbit on your hands.

△ If rabbits and guinea pigs don't gnaw on hard things, their teeth will grow too long. Wooden blocks, one-piece clothespins, or wooden spools for chewing will help keep their teeth in good shape.

enjoy batting things around. Provide a rubber ball, or seal pebbles in a can to make a rattle.

▽ Rabbits and guinea pigs need salt. Buy a block of salt called a salt lick at a pet store. Put it in your pet's cage near the food and water containers.

▷ "A guinea pig is a great pet," says Ryan Jordan. Goldie, a red American guinea pig, often nestles on his shoulder. She greets him with whistles and squeaks, and sits on his lap while he reads. "She'll scamper around the garden if you let her," says Ryan, 12, who lives in Baltimore, Maryland.

N.G.S. PHOTOGRAPHER JOSEPH H. BAILEY

The hair of a Peruvian guinea pig grows 1 inch (2½ cm) a month. Sometimes it's hard to tell which end of the animal is which. The hair should be brushed daily.

JANE BURTON/BRUCE COLEMAN INC.

BREEDS

You may be surprised to find out that North America has 42 domestic rabbit breeds. Some are large. Flemish giants weigh as much as 16 pounds (7 kg). Some are small. Netherland dwarfs weigh as little as 2 pounds (1 kg). Some, called lops, have floppy ears, a little like a hound dog's. Different bunny breeds have different temperaments, too. Some are quiet and easygoing. Others are nervous and fussy.

Guinea pigs today come in seven breeds, each with different fur and markings. Unlike rabbits, most breeds of guinea pigs do not have personalities particular to a breed. Most guinea pigs are sweet-tempered. But that doesn't mean they're all alike. Each guinea pig is likely to have its own lively personality.

△ *Gentle harlequin rabbits were named for their patchwork colors, which reminded people of harlequin clown costumes.*

JANE BURTON/BRUCE COLEMAN LTD. (BELOW AND RIGHT)

△ *The black English spot rabbit is more of a show rabbit than a pet. Breeders look for a velvety coat, a rounded back, and a delicate head.*

▷ *An American guinea pig huddles over her young. The American is the original domestic breed, developed from wild guinea pigs in South America.*

55

Bright-eyed bunnies, as motionless as statues, belong to a breed called Dutch rabbits. Their size, markings, and friendliness have made them the most popular pet rabbit breed. Dutch rabbits also come in pure black, blue, gray, and other colors, including a brown called chocolate Dutch.

56

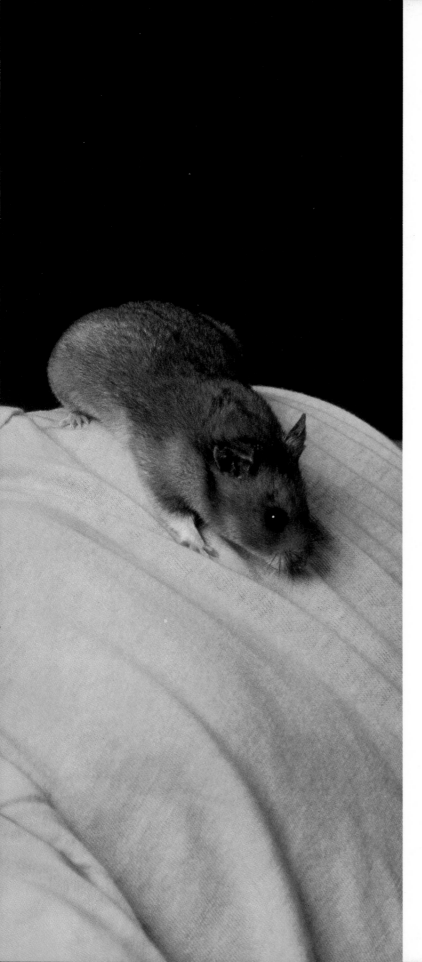

MICE, RATS, HAMSTERS, AND GERBILS

You can probably find some kinds of rodents close to where you live. Rodents include mice, rats, guinea pigs, beavers, squirrels, and quite a few other animals. They all have furry bodies and large front teeth. Some, such as squirrels, don't make good pets. Others, such as mice, rats, hamsters, and gerbils, can make excellent ones.

"Rodents are easy to care for," says Sarah Hall, 10, of Arlington, Virginia. She owns a rat. "You don't have to walk rodents or rescue them from trees. Just give them food and water, keep their cages clean, let them out for exercise, and give them attention."

A glass tank or a wire-mesh cage with a solid bottom makes a good rodent home. Don't use a wooden cage. Your pet will gnaw through it and escape in no time. Keep newspaper on the bottom of the cage, covered with cedar chips or sawdust—or sand, for gerbils. Add tissue, shredded newspaper, cotton, hay, or an old sock for your rodent to use in building a nest.

Clean a mouse cage every day or it will become

◁ *Aaron Dickens didn't have to teach his hamster Mickie to climb around on his back. "Mickie is always looking for something to climb on," says Aaron, 13, of Washington, D. C. "Hamsters are very curious." Aaron ought to know. He's been raising hamsters for six years.*

N.G.S. PHOTOGRAPHER JOSEPH H. BAILEY

59

smelly. Cages of other rodents should be cleaned at least once a week. While cleaning a cage, put your pet in a tightly plugged dry bathtub. If bathers in your house object to that, put your pet in a large can. Watch a rat carefully, however. A rat will climb out of just about anything—except a bathtub.

Vets recommend that you feed a rodent pellets, available at food and pet stores. Add bits of cheese, seeds, raw oatmeal, apple, corn, salad greens, or hard-boiled egg. Don't overdo the extras. Too many vegetables will upset a rodent's digestive system.

Feed your rodent once a day. After the animal has eaten, remove leftover food that might spoil quickly. Provide a gravity water bottle—an upside-down bottle with a spout—and refill it with fresh water daily.

With proper food, housing, and exercise, your rodent should stay healthy. If your pet begins to lose hair, it may have a skin infection or an internal problem. It could be suffering from lack of vitamin C. If you suspect a problem, visit the vet right away.

You can do two things to keep your pet well exercised. First, place an exercise wheel and small boxes and cardboard tubes in the cage. Use your imagination to create a rodent's jungle gym. Second, take your pet out of its cage to play every day.

Rodents are active—and curious as well. Before you let your pet loose in a room, close all doors and cover all floor vents. Don't allow a hamster or a gerbil to run loose on a table. These animals don't see very far. They may run off the edge and injure themselves.

If your pet should escape in your home or outside, try this method of catching it: Place a small paper bag on its side on the floor or the ground with a tempting rodent snack inside it. Your pet may soon scoot right into the bag.

△ *Golden hamsters Greg and Mickie take turns working out on their exercise wheel. Hamsters, rats, mice, and gerbils need a lot of exercise. Give them shelves, ladders, and exercise wheels to play on. This will help keep them from getting bored—and fat.*

60

▽ *Using one of the proper methods of holding a hamster, Aaron grasps his pet around the middle. He holds it firmly but is careful not to squeeze.*

▷ *Sarah Hall, 10, of Arlington, Virginia, cleans her rat's tank with a damp cloth. She changes the bedding once a week. A mouse cage should be cleaned daily.*

TIP-TOP TIPS

△ Rats and mice are famous for climbing. Challenge your own pet rat or mouse. Tie a tightrope no more than 5 inches (13 cm) above its well-padded cage floor.

▷ If you're going to let your rodent out of its cage, tell everyone at home beforehand. Then watch carefully where you and the others walk. It's easy to step on a small pet. Be sure doors stay closed when your pet is out of its cage.

◁ Make a rodent playground. Start with an exercise wheel. Add a clean milk carton in which you have cut a few entrance and exit holes. Glue together a ladder of ice-cream sticks. Make a swing out of a cord and a curtain rod ring. A paper-towel tube makes an excellent tunnel, and an almost-empty cereal box will keep your pet occupied for hours. Change the playground often so that your pet always has new activities.

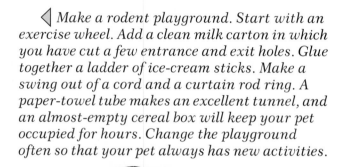

◁ If you own a rodent, you should regularly provide new materials for your pet to sink its teeth into. Rodents need to gnaw to keep their teeth in shape. Here are some ideas for gnawing materials that have other benefits as well. A nearly finished roll of toilet paper shreds into bedding. A beef bone provides calcium for growing rodents. A branch adds to the rodent playground.

▷ Reaching from its clean bed of wood chips, Aaron's hamster Greg takes a fresh treat. Handing a pet snacks and cuddling it helps tame the animal and keep it tame. But handle your pet carefully. A hamster or other rodent may nip your fingers if you frighten it or if your hand smells of food.

N.G.S. PHOTOGRAPHER JOSEPH H. BAILEY

As scientists breed new varieties of rats, they give the breeds names such as Sprague-Dawley and Wistar White. This watchful pet is a Long-Evans black-hooded rat.

N.G.S. PHOTOGRAPHER JOSEPH H. BAILEY

VARIETIES

If you counted the varieties of domestic rats and mice, can you guess how high you'd count? Higher than 700! Rats differ somewhat in size, but mostly in markings, coat quality, and fur color. Mice also differ from each other mostly in markings and fur color.

Why are there so many varieties of mice and rats? It's because humans have bred the varieties. Hamsters and gerbils haven't been domesticated for as long as rats and mice, and you won't find as many varieties of them. There's only one type of gerbil. There are 15 types of hamsters. Only two, the golden and the dwarf, are kept as pets. The pets come in several shades, including tan. Some are striped. One kind of hamster has a thick coat called teddy bear fur.

△ *Carrying one of her babies in her mouth, a golden hamster returns it to her nest. This popular pet was originally found in Syria.*

SU GOODERS/ARDEA LONDON

△ *A pet mouse peers from a favorite spot—a pocket. The many varieties of domesticated mice come in a range of colors.*

▷ *Nursing newborn mice completely fill the nest under their mother. Pet mice are nervous and timid. Handle them with great care and gentleness.*

ANIMALS ANIMALS/RICHARD KOLAR

65

Curious and alert, gerbils represent the newest addition to the pet world. They have been domesticated for only 30 years. Gerbils are livelier than guinea pigs and more sociable than mice. Some people call them pocket kangaroos because they sit up—and leap—much the way kangaroos do.

66

BIRDS

I f you have picked out the kind of bird you want but do not yet have a cage for it, give your choice a lot of thought. Generally, a roomy cage is better for a bird than a small one. The shape of the cage should depend on the kind of bird you plan to put in it.

Parakeets, or budgies, should have a tall cage. They tend to climb up and down. Provide a ladder for parakeets to climb on. Canaries are active fliers. Provide them with a wide cage. Cockatiels and other parrots should have a cage that is both tall and wide. They need room to flap their long wings.

Your next job is to find the best location for your bird cage. Drafts or cold air from a window—even a closed one—can give the bird a cold. Too much direct sunlight can kill a bird. However, a bird should have some sunlight. Living in natural light helps keep a bird in tune with the seasons. Like plants, healthy birds have a seasonal growing cycle.

When placing your bird cage, remember that birds scatter seeds in a wide circle outside their cages. It's

◁ *Two pet cockatiels, with the upturned crests, and a pair of parakeets try out new perches. Their owners, Dawn Milligan, 11, and her brother, Allen, 13, built the perches from a kit they bought in a pet store. Try perches at different heights and angles. You'll soon see what's right for your bird.*

best not to put a cage over a shaggy rug. Many cages come with side panels that prevent most seeds from scattering. You can buy a plastic or cloth device to hang around the base of a cage to catch seeds.

Put a variety of perches in the cage. A natural branch makes an excellent perch. The various thicknesses of a branch let the bird choose the thickness it wants. And the rough bark will help keep the bird's claws trim. Be careful to place perches far enough from the walls of the cage so that a bird has tail room and space to flap its wings. Perches should be near, but not over, the food and water dishes.

Line the cage with newspaper and change the paper twice a week. Use your judgment about how often to replace branches, but scrub the perches and cage once a week. Wash the food and water dishes every few days. A dirty cage will make your bird sick.

Canaries, finches, parakeets, and parrots depend mainly on seeds for food. Keep your bird's food dish full of birdseed at all times. Check the dish to make sure it contains seeds, and not just empty shells and husks. Blow lightly on the dish and the empty seed shells will blow out, leaving the full ones.

Fresh, well-washed fruits, vegetables, and greens are a good source of vitamins and minerals. Bits of yolk from a hard-boiled egg provide important protein. Offer these foods to your bird a little at a time. Watch to see which ones the bird likes best, and which it doesn't like. Always remove leftover food that would soon spoil.

Observe a bird as it eats. You'll see that it doesn't chew. It swallows its food whole. Among seed-eating birds, gravel in the crop, or gizzard—part of the digestive system—helps grind up the food. A bird needs to keep renewing its gravel supply. To help the bird do

△ *Breeders usually start taming birds a few hours after they hatch to get them used to people. Let your bird get used to your hand in its cage before you hold it. Don't touch wild baby birds in their nests. Their parents may abandon them.*

▷ *Wire screening lets fresh air into a large bird cage called an aviary. Your bird's home may be much smaller, but it, too, should provide fresh air—without drafts.*

70

▷ *Though its name isn't Polly, this African gray parrot does eat an occasional cracker. It regularly eats sunflower seeds, peanuts, fruit, and corn and other fresh vegetables. If properly handled, parrots can be affectionate pets. However, use caution with all parrots. They have powerful beaks and can bite very hard.*

this, put a container of bird gravel next to the food.

Every so often, your bird will begin to shed its feathers and grow new ones. This is called molting. All birds molt. Some lose many feathers at once. For a while, they look rather shaggy. Other birds lose and replace feathers so gradually that you may not even notice. When your bird molts, pay special attention to its diet. A bird needs plenty of vitamins and minerals to produce new feathers. Add a few drops—but just a few—of cod-liver oil or vitamins A and D to the seed.

If your bird is tame, give it plenty of opportunity to keep you company out of its cage. But keep an eye on it. Parrots, for example, will try to eat almost anything. And all pet birds must be protected from cats.

▽ *A parrot weighs in during a checkup at the vet's. Birds don't need regular visits, but check with a vet if your bird seems ill. Runny eyes, noisy breathing, and ruffled feathers may indicate illness.*

◁ *A parakeet cracks shells and swallows the seeds inside whole. Seedeaters, which include most pet birds, must eat fine gravel with their seeds. It helps grind up food inside their bodies. If your bird food doesn't come with gravel, place a dish of it in the cage.*

△ As she does every day, Dawn changes her pets' food and water. Birds are very active. They have to eat almost all of the time they're not resting. Make sure your bird always has food. When you check the food dish, don't be fooled by empty seed husks. Be sure the dish contains plenty of whole seeds. Give a pet bird a cuttlebone like the one on the left side of the cage. Birds sharpen their beaks on the cuttlebone and swallow small bits of it. It contains calcium, a mineral that keeps birds' beaks and bones strong.

73

TIP-TOP TIPS

▷ If your bird likes to bathe, make it a once-a-week routine. For most birds, place a shallow clay dish of water in the cage. After your bird has splashed around for a while, remove the dish. If you have a parrot, give it a shower once a week with a plant mister.

△ Look around your home. It's full of good bird toys. Buttons, bells, and paper clips tied to twine that's dangling in the cage will keep a bird occupied for hours. Never leave loose string lying where your bird can reach it. A bird can easily tangle itself up.

▷ Train your bird to sing, whistle, or talk. Parakeets and parrots may learn to say a few words. Male canaries may sing tunes. The trick is to start when a bird is young. Repeat a word or a tune, or whistle over and over, for a short period every day. You can buy a training record at a pet store if you get tired of repeating your lessons. When your pet has learned a few phrases or tunes, have it perform for your friends.

HELLO...

▽ Does your bird wake you with a song too early in the morning? Put a cloth cover over the bird's cage at night. Your bird won't start singing in the morning until you remove the cover.

▷ Cookie, a male cockatiel, stares at his reflection. A lone bird seems to think it has company when it sees its reflection. For this reason, owners often hang small mirrors in bird cages. Male canaries that have never sung before have burst into song after seeing themselves in a mirror for the first time.

DAVE HORNBACK

A yellow face on a cockatiel tells you the bird is a male. A female would have a gray face. The cockatiel, a kind of parrot, can be trained to whistle and talk. It makes an affectionate pet.

KIM TAYLOR & JANE BURTON/BRUCE COLEMAN LTD.

ANIMALS ANIMALS/BRECK P. KENT

SPECIES

Domesticated birds provide a wide variety of characteristics to choose from. Before picking a bird, consider what you want most: A cheery song? A male canary might be best. A bird easily tamed? Look at a parakeet. A companion? Any pet bird will do!

At one time, many birds sold in pet stores and markets had been caught in the wild. A lot of birds died while being trapped or shipped. Others died after they were sold. Many countries now have laws that protect wild birds. Most of the birds you can buy today were raised in captivity. They are usually healthier and tamer than birds caught in the wild. When considering a pet bird, make sure it's one that was bred in captivity, and not one that was captured.

△ *The canary gets its name from the Canary Islands, where the bird was first found. Most male canaries sing; females chirp.*

MARK S. CARLSON/TOM STACK & ASSOCIATES

△ *Parakeets, also called budgies, are the most popular pet birds. If trained when very young, a parakeet can learn to talk.*

▷ *A yellow-naped Amazon parrot ruffles its feathers to dry off. Parrots live a long time, sometimes more than 60 years.*

JANE BURTON/BRUCE COLEMAN INC.

77

△ *Little larger than a sparrow, the diamond dove is a recent addition to the world of pet birds. It originally lived in the wild in Australia. Breeders now raise it in aviaries all over the world.*

▷ *The fantail pigeon comes from India, where it is sold in marketplaces. This pigeon is a favorite at bird shows in North America. Breeders look for a small head and a neck that is long and thin when extended. The tail should be flat and circular.*

FISH

If you are new to the world of aquariums, you'll have to decide right away whether you want a freshwater aquarium or a marine aquarium. Because marine, or saltwater, aquariums are difficult to keep, this chapter will consider only freshwater tanks.

In addition to an aquarium, you will need an air pump, a filter system, a heater, a thermometer, lights, aquarium gravel, and plants. The tank will need a lid to limit evaporation, to hold lights, to keep dust from falling in, and to prevent lively fish from jumping out.

Keep in mind that once you fill a tank, you probably won't be able to move it. Choose its location before you fill it. Place the aquarium on a strong stand or shelf. Make sure there is an electrical outlet nearby. Don't choose a sunny spot or one too close to a radiator or heat vent. Sunlight can heat the water, killing the fish. It will also cause algae—tiny plants—to grow and cloud the water.

Prepare your tank before you buy fish. Lay down a bed of well-rinsed gravel. Put the thermometer where

◁ *A fish called a Jack Dempsey hovers near its eggs as Krista Beattie wags her finger to attract it. Krista, 13, of Woodstock, Ontario, in Canada, spends about two hours a week taking care of her fish. She spends many more hours just watching them. "Every time you look in the tank, you see a different picture," she says.*
STEVEN BEHAL

81

you can read it. Place the air pump, the heater, and the filter at the rear of the tank and hook them up according to the directions on the packages.

Now add the water. Pour it slowly down the inside of the tank so you don't stir up the gravel. Or place a small dish on the gravel and let water flow through a hose onto the dish. When the tank is about two-thirds full, root the plants in the gravel. Then fill the tank to within 3 inches (7½ cm) of the top.

Here comes the hard part. You have to let the water stand for a week before putting fish into it. Most tap water contains chlorine, which kills fish. As you let water stand, the chlorine evaporates. Never expose fish to water that has not aged.

Don't overcrowd your aquarium. Plan to have at least a half gallon (2 L) of water for each inch of fish. That means, for example, that if you have a two-inch fish and a four-inch fish, you'll have six inches of fish and need at least 3 gallons (12 L). You may wish to include a catfish and some snails. They eat algae and fish waste, helping to keep your tank clean.

Along with a pinch of fish flakes twice a day, feed your fish fresh food. Ask at a pet shop for tubifex worms, brine shrimp, or water fleas, called daphnia. If your fish are still eating five minutes after you feed them, give them a bit less food in the future.

STEVEN BEHAL (ALL)

▷ *With her father standing by, Krista introduces new fish into her tank. She floats the fish—bag and all—in the tank for about 30 minutes. Gradually, the water in the bag becomes the same temperature as the surrounding water. Then Krista releases the fish.*

◁ *Just a pinch of flake food and brine shrimp or tiny worms is all Krista gives her fish—twice a day. Don't overfeed the fish in your tank. Too much food can kill them.*

▷ *Krista regularly wipes off the inside walls of the tank and removes waste, dead plants, and uneaten food. You should clean your tank once a week.*

TIP-TOP TIPS

◁ Create a small forest of plants in one or two places in your aquarium. Young fish, called fry, may live safely among the plants until they are large enough to protect themselves.

△ Interesting surroundings may help keep your fish lively and healthy. Put well-rinsed plants, shells, and rocks with holes through them in the aquarium.

▷ When you buy new aquarium plants, first rinse them in salt water to kill any germs. Then rinse them again in fresh water to clean off the salt before putting them into the tank.

▽ Don't tap on the glass to attract the attention of your fish. Tapping may disturb them and send them swimming for cover. It's best simply to watch them. To see the shyest ones, wait until feeding time, when they'll swim into view.

△ Has one of your fish changed color, developed spots, lost its appetite, or started to move slowly? If it's ill, it could infect other fish. Set up a separate hospital tank to isolate the sick fish until it gets better.

△ Attach feeding rings at opposite ends of your tank at the water surface. When you sprinkle food into the rings, the fish will feed in limited areas. The food won't spread across the tank and sink unnoticed to the bottom.

TAP! TAP!

Discus fish come from the Amazon River, in South America. They need so much extra care that only experts should keep them.

HANS REINHARD/BRUCE COLEMAN INC. (ABOVE, AND BELOW RIGHT)

SPECIES

Many varieties of tropical fish get along well together. If you put several different kinds of fish into one tank, you will have a colorful collection called a community tank.

For a community tank, choose fish species that have about the same temperature requirements and that will live together peacefully. Visit a pet store to find out which fish are appropriate for a community tank. You'll have a big choice of color, size, and shape.

Different kinds of fish tend to live at different levels of a tank. Catfish feed around the aquarium floor. Angelfish swim mostly at the middle level. Gouramis and guppies usually stay near the surface. For the most lively tank, plan to have fish at each level.

△ *Angelfish often grow quite large. Popular and hardy pets, they do well in tanks with a variety of other tropical fish.*

P. MORRIS/ARDEA LONDON

△ *Lively cardinal tetras are healthiest—and most dramatic to watch—when kept in groups. Their deep red color fades at night.*

▷ *Goldfish are probably the most common aquarium fish. They may also be the easiest to own. You can keep them inside, or in ponds outdoors year-round.*

Colorful and peaceful, rainbowfish are ideal for a community tank. In the wild, rainbowfish live in freshwater lakes and streams in Australia. In an aquarium, they should be kept with a fair amount of plant life. They usually swim at the middle level of a tank among well-spaced leafy plants.

HORSES AND PONIES

If you are about to become the new owner of a horse, have a vet check it thoroughly before you buy it. Interview the previous owners if possible. Can they tell you about any likes or dislikes the horse has? How often did they ride it? Change the animal's routine as little as possible in the first months you own it.

Walk your horse in its new surroundings. Let it get used to animals, clotheslines near its enclosure, and other sights that might startle it. And don't ride it on its first day at home.

A horse should have an acre or more of pasture for grazing and exercise. If it can't have that much space, it should at least have a sizable grassy area called a paddock next to its shelter. Enclose the paddock or pasture with a board fence or a fence of boards and smooth wire. (Barbed wire could cut a horse.)

In most climates, a barn is not absolutely necessary. But a horse does need shelter from the sun and from heavy storms. With an adult's help, you can build a simple but sturdy three-sided stall, or convert

◁ *Staying close to its mother, a young horse canters across a pasture. The young Morgan, called a foal, still has its fluffy baby coat. In its first months, the foal seems to be made mostly of legs. Over the summer, its body will grow and catch up with its legs.*

an old toolshed into a shelter for your pet. The shelter should have a high ceiling and a wood or dirt floor with proper drainage. A concrete floor would be too hard on your horse's feet. Cover the floor with wood chips or straw. Water should be available in the shelter whenever the horse is shut in. Also keep a water trough filled in the pasture or paddock.

Horses eat three basic foods: grasses, hay, and a mixture of grains and molasses called sweet feed. The amount of each will depend on the season, on the animal's size, and on how much exercise the animal gets. Ask your vet or someone from a pony club to advise you on your pet's needs. Don't overfeed. Overfed horses become too frisky to ride—or they become ill. Keep grain stored out of your animal's reach.

A horse's routine should vary with the season. During each season, however, it should be the same every day. In winter, shut your horse in at night. In spring and fall, you may leave the animal out most of the time, but not during heavy rains or in high winds. In summer, leave the horse out unless the weather is too hot or horseflies are biting badly.

Groom your horse daily with a stiff brush, then clean out its hooves with a pick. Speak gently to it as you work and don't make sudden moves. While grooming, check for cuts and swellings. Simple cuts left untended may develop into infections.

Whenever you set out on a ride, start slowly. Let the horse's muscles warm up. Shortly before you return, ride slowly again. If the horse or pony is sweaty when you get back, lead it around at a walk until it cools off. Don't let it drink while it's still hot and sweaty, or it may become sick. Once your pet has cooled off, use a cloth to rub the animal's coat where the saddle and bridle have left marks. Finally, give your pal a pat.

△ *Danyelle Gardner, 14, of Purcellville, Virginia, cleans out her horse's hoof with a tool called a pick. She cleans Cherokee's hooves after each ride. "If it isn't done regularly, a horse could develop diseased hooves," says Danyelle.*

90

▽ *Danyelle checks the saddle to make sure it is tightly secured by the girth, the leather strap that fastens around a horse's belly. Cherokee is tied by a lead line clipped to his halter.*

▷ *Ira Brackett, 13, of Rogerson, Idaho, and his horse, Hardy, head after a stray steer. Ira's western saddle is designed to hold the rider securely and comfortably during long rides.*

TIP-TOP TIPS

◁ A horse can look forward and backward without turning its head. To know which way your horse is looking as you ride, watch its ears. The ears always point in the direction the horse is looking.

▷ When bridling your horse on cold days, warm the bit with your hands before slipping it into the animal's mouth. A cold bit makes an uncomfortable mouthful.

▷ Keep your fingers and palm as flat as possible when giving a horse a treat. Otherwise the horse may mistake a finger or a thumb for part of the snack. Ouch!

▽ Letting your horse graze on too much spring grass may make it sick. In the early spring, turn your horse out for only a few hours a day. As the weeks go by, you can let it stay out for longer and longer periods of time.

△ Watch where your horse puts its feet. Make sure it doesn't plant one on top of one of yours. If a horse does step on your foot, lean hard against the animal's side. The horse should shift its weight, freeing your foot.

▷ Danyelle scratches Cherokee under his halter as he nuzzles her face. You don't always have to be riding to enjoy owning a horse or pony. On pleasant days, bring a book out to the paddock or pasture for a quiet hour or two. Your pet will appreciate your company.

J. SHERWOOD CHALMERS

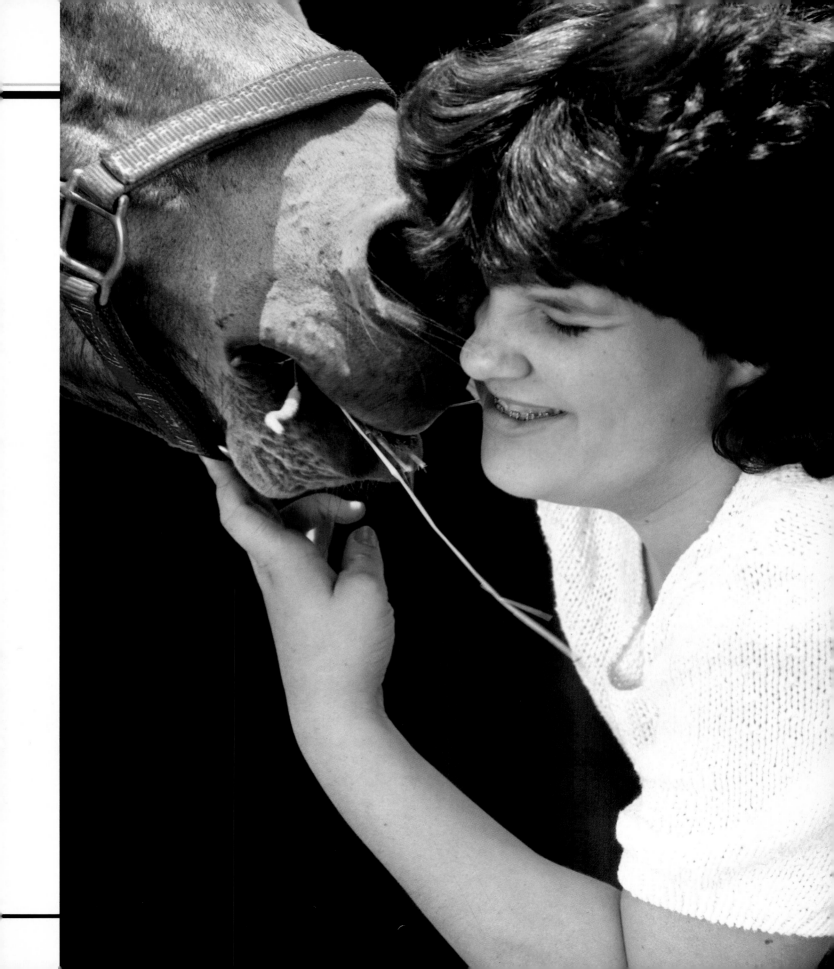

The popular Welsh mountain pony is an intelligent animal. The breed is trained to pull light carts, to hunt, to jump, and even to help lightweight cowhands round up cattle.

JEAN-PAUL FERRERO/ARDEA LONDON

BREEDS

When you think of a horse, do you picture a race horse? A circus pony? There are dozens of horse breeds, and they vary greatly in size. The Shire, an English farm horse, stands as tall at the shoulder as the roof of a full-size van. The Falabella, first bred in Argentina, grows only to about the size of a collie.

All horse and pony breeds belong to a single animal species: the horse. The difference between horses and ponies is merely size. Experts measure a horse's height in hands. One hand equals 4 inches (10 cm). Measure your horse from the ground to its withers—the top of its shoulders. As a general rule, if a horse is $14\frac{2}{10}$ hands or less, it is a pony. At $14\frac{3}{10}$ hands or more, the animal is a horse.

△ Strong, patient, and gentle, Shetland ponies are easy to keep. They are the most popular saddle ponies for beginning riders.

ANIMALS ANIMALS/ROBERT MAIER

△ The Clydesdale, a large and heavy horse, was bred in Scotland for hauling wagons and for other farm work. The long, silky hairs on its legs are called feathers.

▷ Like many riding horses, this is a grade horse, or crossbreed. Some mixes of horses make better riding horses than others. Check with experts before buying one.

STEPHEN GREEN-ARMYTAGE

A silky mane, a head and tail carried high, a gracefully curved neck, and light, dancing paces mean that this horse is an Arabian. The Arabian was bred in the deserts of the Arabian Peninsula. It has a small stomach and needs less food and water than other horses its size.

4

YOU DON'T HAVE TO OWN IT

You're standing on the playground with your young pet raccoon on your shoulders. An admiring crowd of friends gathers round. Who hasn't dreamed of having such a pet? Unfortunately, in real life, the cute raccoon grows up and begins to scratch and hiss. You have to set it free in the woods—where it may not survive.

Or maybe you own a boa constrictor. It gets sick, and no vet in your area treats snakes. Or your pet baby alligator grows too big and toothy, and you don't know *what* to do with it.

The reality of owning a wild animal as a pet is very different from the dream. For one thing, wild creatures are wild. They haven't been domesticated. Though a wild animal may be friendly when young, wild characteristics usually appear as it grows older. Another problem is that unusual animals require unusual care. Often they become sicker and sicker in captivity, with their unhappy

◁ *This orange-kneed tarantula (tuh-RAN-chuh-luh) lives in the Insect Zoo at the Museum of Natural History, in Washington, D. C. Thousands of visitors see spiders and insects there every year. Visitors may handle several of the insects.*

▷ *To many people, the raccoon is a cute, cuddly creature. But remember: It's a wild animal. Like most other wild creatures, it may scratch and bite in captivity and it may carry diseases. It's safest to leave raccoons where they're best off—in the wild.*

owners watching helplessly, not knowing what to do.

There are ways you can enjoy wild animals close up—and unfamiliar domesticated animals, too—without owning them. Many programs introduce people to animals. An expert might visit your classroom with a wild animal such as a snake or an owl. At a petting zoo, you might stroke a llama. At an insect zoo, you might hold a huge grasshopper or a giant cockroach. Turn to page 102 for a list of animal programs.

If you can't have a pet at home, but you want to have the experience of caring for an animal, talk with a teacher about getting a classroom pet or starting a class zoo. Many students keep rabbits or guinea pigs in their classrooms. They divide the responsibilities and share the fun of taking care of the class pets.

If you want an animal, but only for a little while, try keeping a short-term pet. Animals such as water bugs, earthworms, caterpillars, lightning bugs, and tadpoles make fascinating temporary pets. Don't keep more than one or two at a time. And, except for tadpoles and caterpillars, don't keep them more than 48 hours. These creatures are difficult to feed properly.

When collecting a small animal from the wild, always gather part of the environment in which you found it. Take some earth for the earthworm, some pond water for the tadpole, and so on.

Most tadpoles, when they grow legs and become frogs, toads, or salamanders, will need to climb out of the water to breathe. Make sure you place a rock that pokes above the water in your pet's tank or jar.

When it's time to let your part-time pet go, take it back to the area where you found it and set it gently on the ground or in the water. Don't be tempted to keep it for long. Remain a short-term zookeeper. That's being responsible toward wild animals.

▷ *As part of a program called Kids 'N' Critters, Gayle Richards shows Aaron Milburn and Robin Bell, both 6, how a snake specialist handles a boa constrictor. The program of the Animal Welfare League of Arlington, Virginia, allows youngsters to meet wild animals without buying them.*

◁ *For a short-term pet, collect a tadpole—and some of the water in which you found it. Add pond plants to its tank. After it grows legs and climbs out of the water, release it where you found it.*

▷ *Eight-year-olds Andy Reams and Tommy Zipf, of Webster Groves, Missouri, spend a quiet moment with their class pet. The boys and their classmates take turns caring for the rabbit.*

ANIMAL PROGRAMS FOR YOU

If you'd like to become further involved with wild or domestic animals, look through this list. Contact one of the organizations near you for more information.

ZOO PROGRAMS

1. Little Rock Zoological Gardens, 1 Jonesboro Drive, Little Rock, Ark. 72205. "Walk on the Wild Side!" Zoo Adventure Classes. Ages 4 and up. Various one-day classes in June. Get acquainted with the zoo's touchable animals and learn basics of zookeeping.

2. Santa Barbara Zoological Gardens, 500 Ninos Drive, Santa Barbara, Cal. 93103.
   A. Zoo Day Camp. Ages 3–11. Behind-the-scenes demonstrations. Three-week sessions throughout summer.
   B. Junior Zookeeper Program. Ages 12–17. Offers chance to work in zoo and to study animal care and behavior.
   C. Foster Feeder Program. Youngsters "adopt" zoo animal as pet by paying for food for one year. Fees: $25 and up.

3. National Zoological Park, Smithsonian Institution, Washington, D.C. 20008.
   Herpetology Learning Center. Herplab open every day. Summer, 10–6; winter, 10–4:30. Docents teach zoology through activities built around living things, natural objects.

4. Zoological Society of Florida, 12400 S.W. 152nd St., Miami, Fla. 33177.
   A. Adopt-an-Animal Program. Youngsters of all ages. Adopt animals: birds to elephants. Fees: $25 to $2,500 a year.
   B. Jungle Juniors Day Camp. Grades 1–3. Week-long day sessions during summer.
   C. Zoo Camp. Grades 4–6. Week-long full-day sessions. Tour zoo behind the scenes. Friday lunch with zookeeper.

5. Audubon Zoological Garden, P.O. Box 4327, New Orleans, La. 70178.
   A. Junior Zookeeper Program. 7th and 8th graders. One-year commitment to participate. Volunteers work throughout school year helping with zookeeping chores, public education programs.
   B. Audubon Zoomobile. Docents take wild animals for educational presentations to physically and mentally handicapped groups in hospitals, special education classes, camps.
   C. Adopt-an-Audubon-Animal Program. Participants become Zoo Parents by helping pay for special diet and care of favorite zoo animal for one year. Fees start at $15.
   D. Wisner Children's Village: In special area of zoo, youngsters come face-to-face with zoo animals and try out animal-related activities such as walking through Endangered Species Maze.

6. Metro Toronto Zoo, P.O. Box 280, West Hill, Ontario, Canada M1E 4R5. Ages 5 and up. Littlefoot Club: special zoo tours, newsletter. Adopt-an-Animal Program. Fees help buy animals' food.

7. Zoological Society of Philadelphia, 34th St. and Girard Avenue, Philadelphia, Pa. 19104.
   A. Zoo-2-U Program. Docents in zoo van take live animals to classrooms in area schools. Weekday mornings. Teachers should contact Philadelphia Board of Education Science Office.
   B. Close Encounters. Youngsters of all ages. Call zoo to arrange special tour. Docents stationed at major houses of zoo.
   C. Zoo Camp. Ages 6–12. Week-long summer day camp provides ecology-oriented experiences in zoo classrooms.
   D. Junior Zoo Intern Program. Ages 11–13. Summer day camp for adolescents. Four-week sessions in July and August.

8. Oglebay's Good Children's Zoo, Wheeling, W.Va. 26003.
   A. Docent program. Ages 12–16. After training and testing, volunteers help zookeepers with all aspects of zoo care.
   B. Zoo Discovery Day Camp. Ages 8–12. Youngsters study and handle insects, spiders, various wild and domestic animals.

INSECT ZOOS

1. Arizona-Sonora Desert Museum, Route 9, Box 900, Tucson, Ariz. 85743. Summer, 7 to sundown; winter, 8:30 to sundown.
2. San Francisco Zoological Society Insect Zoo, Sloat and Skyline Blvds., San Francisco, Cal. 94132. Open every day. Summer, 10:30–4:30; winter, 11–4. Call for demonstrations.
3. Smithsonian Insect Zoo, Natural History Building, 10th St. and Constitution Ave. N.W., Washington, D.C. 20560. Open every day, 10–5:30. Fifty exhibits.
4. Cincinnati Zoo Insectarium, Insect World, 3400 Vine St., Cincinnati, Oh. 45220. Open every day. Summer, 10–7; winter, 10–5. Call to arrange for volunteer to give demonstrations.

AQUARIUMS

1. Vancouver Aquarium, P.O. Box 3232, Vancouver, British Columbia, Canada V6B 3X8. Ages 8 and up. One-day workshops.
2. Marineland, 6610 Palos Verdes Drive South, Rancho Palos Verdes, Cal. 90274. One-day programs. Reservations required.
3. Sea Life Park, Makapuu Point, Waimanalo, Oahu, Ha. 96795. Pre-school and up. One-day to week-long programs year-round.
4. John G. Shedd Aquarium, 1200 South Lake Shore Drive, Chicago, Ill. 60605. Programs throughout year. Kindergarten and up.
5. National Aquarium, Pier 3, 501 East Pratt St., Baltimore, Md. 21202. Grades 4–6. Programs of 1–3 days throughout summer.

HUMANE EDUCATION PROGRAMS

1. Marin Humane Society, 171 Bel Marin Keys Boulevard, Novato, Cal. 94947. Junior Volunteer program. Ages 9–15. Upon completion, youngsters qualify as volunteers in local kennels.
2. Indianapolis Humane Society, 7929 North Michigan Road, Indianapolis, Ind. 46268. Ages 6–12. Kindness Club meets once a month. Youngsters work with shelter animals. Also, Kindness Day Camp. Ages 6–12. Four one-week sessions during summer.
3. The Animal Rescue League of Boston, P.O. Box 265, Boston, Mass. 02117. Animal Friends Summer Day Camp. Kindergarten graduates through age 13. Three-week session in July, four-week session in August. On shores of Buzzards Bay, Massachusetts.
4. Animal Welfare League of Arlington, 2650 South Arlington Mill Drive, Arlington, Va. 22206. Kind Kids 'N' Critters Program. Three programs for ages 5–12. Late July through August.
5. Wisconsin Humane Society, 4151 N. Humboldt Ave., Milwaukee, Wis. 53212. Animal Awareness Day Camp. Ages 8–11. Separate one-week sessions in July. Field trips, guest speakers.

MISCELLANEOUS PROGRAMS

1. Sierra Club, 530 Bush St., San Francisco, Cal. 94108. Youngsters of all ages. Learn about wild animals' roles in nature by participating with parents in summer family camping expeditions.
2. National Audubon Society Summer Youth Ecology Camp, c/o Marshal Case, N.E. Audubon Center, Rte. 1, Box 171, Sharon, Conn. 06069. Ages 10–14. One-week sessions.
3. National Park Service, Department of the Interior, P.O. Box 37127, Washington, D.C. 20013-7127. Junior Ranger Programs. Local branches of National Park Service across the United States sponsor hands-on programs taught by rangers. Participants learn about and observe animals in the wild. Junior Rangers receive certificates upon completion of a program, and then volunteer time to Park Service.
4. National Wildlife Federation, 1412 16th St. N.W., Washington, D.C. 20036. Youngsters join Ranger Rick's Discovery Club, a classroom or neighborhood club. Ages 3–13. With an adult leader, members participate in such activities as studying pond life, building bird houses, and creating backyard wildlife sanctuaries.
5. Oxon Hill Working Farm, c/o National Capitol Parks East, 1900 Anacostia Dr. S.E., Washington, D.C. 20020. Every day, 8:30–5. Supervised farm-oriented activities.
6. Wolf Sanctuary, P.O. Box 760, Eureka, Mo. 63035. Youngsters of all ages. Lectures, guided tours through Wolf Sanctuary. Call for reservations.

INDEX

Bold type refers to illustrations or map; regular type refers to text.

ADDITIONAL READING

For more information about a particular kind of pet, look in a library, pet store, or bookstore for one of these books: *Understanding Your Pet,* by Dr. Michael W. Fox (Coward, McCann, and Geoghegan, N.Y., 1978); *Great Pets,* by Sara Stein (Workman Publishing Co., Inc., N.Y., 1976); or *Pets, Every Owner's Encyclopedia,* (Paddington Press, N.Y., 1978). You might also consult a book from one of the following series.

• "A Complete Owner's Manual" series (Barron's Educational Series, Inc., Woodbury, N.Y.) includes books on hamsters, gerbils, cockatiels, cats, parrots, spaniels, poodles, snakes, rabbits, guinea pigs, long-haired cats, and on dogs in general.

• "How to Raise and Train A . . ." series (TFH Publications, Inc., Neptune City, N.J.) includes books on Brittany spaniels, Chihuahuas, cocker spaniels, collies, Great Pyrenees, greyhounds, Irish setters, Rottweilers, and other dogs. TFH Publications also has books on bettas, long-haired and Siamese cats, chameleons, frogs, gerbils, goldfish, guinea pigs, guppies, kittens, mice, rabbits, rats, salamanders, snakes, and teddy bear hamsters.

• "Junior Petkeeper's Library" series (Franklin Watts, London) includes books on cats, dogs, fish, gerbils, guinea pigs, hamsters, mice, rabbits, and rats.

• "Know . . ." series and "Enjoy . . ." series (Pet Library Ltd., Harrison, N.J.) include books on canaries, dog grooming and training, fish breeding, goldfish, killifish, Siamese cats, parakeets, Persian cats, poodles, and tropical fish diseases.

EDUCATIONAL CONSULTANTS

Michael W. Fox, D.Sc., Ph.D., B. Vet. Med. MRCVS, Scientific Director, Institute for the Study of Animal Problems, The Humane Society of the United States, Washington, D. C., *Chief Consultant*

Glenn O. Blough, LL.D., Emeritus Professor of Education, University of Maryland, *Educational Consultant*

Nicholas J. Long, Ph.D., *Consulting Psychologist*

Joan Myers, Alexandria City Public Schools, *Reading Consultant*

The Special Publications and School Services Division is also grateful to the individuals and institutions named or quoted in the text and to those cited here for their generous assistance:

Beverly Armstrong, Kids 'N' Critters; Michael Bailey, National Aquarium, Washington, D. C.; Marna S. Fogarty, Cat Fanciers' Association; Arthur Freud, *American Cage-Bird Magazine;* Pam Granderson, American Harlequin Rabbit Club; Teresa M. Kohl, American Horse Council; Maxine D. and Robert W. Leishman, Rocky Mountain Cavy Club, American Cavy Breeders Association; Penny F. Miller, Garrison Forest School, Garrison, Maryland; The National Association for the Advancement of Humane Education; Stanley J. Olsen, University of Arizona; Gerald T. Padgett, Kingman Boys and Girls Club, Washington, D. C.; Kathie Pontikes, The Miriam School, Webster Groves, Missouri; Kathleen Savesky, Massachusetts SPCA, Framingham; Joan Spade, The Humane Society of the United States; Ann Squire, ASPCA; Pets Are Wonderful Council, Chicago; Melinda A. Zeder, Smithsonian Institution.

Composition for YOUR WORLD OF PETS by National Geographic's Photographic Services, Carl M. Shrader, Director; Lawrence F. Ludwig, Assistant Director. Printed and bound by Holladay-Tyler Printing Corp., Rockville, Md. Color separations by the Lanman-Progressive Co., Washington, D. C.; Lincoln Graphics, Inc., Cherry Hill, N.J.; NEC, Inc., Nashville, Tenn. FAR-OUT FUN! printed by McCollum Press, Inc., Rockville, Md. *Classroom Activities* produced by Mazer Corp., Dayton, Ohio.

Library of Congress CIP Data

McGrath, Susan, 1955-
    Your world of pets.
    (Books for world explorers)
    Bibliography: p.
    Includes index.
    Summary: Describes the wild ancestors of modern pets, how to choose a suitable pet, and how to care for eleven different kinds, including dogs, cats, rabbits, gerbils, fish, and horses.
    1. Pets—Juvenile literature. [1. Pets]
I. Gibson, Barbara, ill. II. Title. III. Series.
SF416.2.M32   1985   636.08'87   85-7288
ISBN 0-87044-517-0
ISBN 0-87044-522-7 (lib. bdg.)

YOUR WORLD OF PETS

by Susan McGrath

PUBLISHED BY
THE NATIONAL GEOGRAPHIC SOCIETY
WASHINGTON, D. C.

Gilbert M. Grosvenor, *President*
Melvin M. Payne, *Chairman of the Board*
Owen R. Anderson, *Executive Vice President*
Robert L. Breeden, *Vice President,
Publications and Educational Media*

PREPARED BY THE SPECIAL PUBLICATIONS
AND SCHOOL SERVICES DIVISION

Donald J. Crump, *Director*
Philip B. Silcott, *Associate Director*
William L. Allen, *Assistant Director*

BOOKS FOR WORLD EXPLORERS
Pat Robbins, *Editor*
Ralph Gray, *Editor Emeritus*
Margaret McKelway, *Associate Editor*
Ursula Perrin Vosseler, *Art Director*

STAFF FOR *YOUR WORLD OF PETS*
Roger B. Hirschland, *Managing Editor*
Jane R. McGoldrick, *Contributing Editor*
Alison Wilbur Eskildsen, *Picture Editor*
Mary Elizabeth Molloy, *Designer*
M. Barbara Brownell, *Researcher*
Suzanne Nave Patrick, *Contributing Researcher*
Barbara L. Gibson, *Artist*
Lori Elizabeth Davie, *Editorial Assistant*
Bernadette L. Grigonis, Artemis S. Lampathakis,
Illustrations Assistants
Janet A. Dustin, *Art Secretary*

STAFF FOR *FAR-OUT FUN!*: Patricia N. Holland, *Project Editor;* Martha C. Christian, Catherine O'Neill, *Text Editors;* Mary Elizabeth Molloy, *Designer;* M. Barbara Brownell, *Researcher;* Beverly Armstrong, *Artist*

ENGRAVING, PRINTING, AND PRODUCT MANUFACTURE: Robert W. Messer, *Manager;* George V. White, *Production Manager;* Mary A. Bennett, *Production Project Manager;* Mark R. Dunlevy, David V. Showers, Gregory Storer, George J. Zeller, Jr., *Assistant Production Managers;* Julia F. Warner, *Production Staff Assistant*

STAFF ASSISTANTS: Elizabeth A. Brazerol, Dianne T. Craven, Carol R. Curtis, Mary Elizabeth Davis, Ann Di Fiore, Eva A. Dillon, Rosamund Garner, Anne Hampford, Virginia W. Hannasch, Nancy J. Harvey, Joan Hurst, Katherine R. Leitch, Cleo Petroff, Pamela Black Townsend, Virginia A. Williams, Eric Wilson

MARKET RESEARCH: Mark W. Brown, Joseph S. Fowler, Carrla L. Holmes, Meg M. Kieffer, Barbara Steinwurtzel, Marsha Sussman, Judy Turnbull

INDEX: Dianne L. H. Hardy